grade

Prompt, Plan, Write!

Practice for FIVE types of writing...

- Descriptive writing
- Personal narratives
- Imaginative narratives
- Persuasive writing
- Expository writing

...and more than a DOZEN different writing skills!

Written by Kim Minafo

Managing Editor: Amy Payne

Editorial Team: Becky S. Andrews, Kimberley Bruck, Sharon Murphy, Debra Liverman, Diane Badden, Thad H. McLaurin, Jennifer Bragg, Karen A. Brudnak, Juli Docimo Blair, Hope Rodgers, Dorothy C. McKinney

Production Team: Lori Z. Henry, Pam Crane, Rebecca Saunders, Chris Curry, Sarah Foreman, Theresa Lewis Goode, Greg D. Rieves, Eliseo De Jesus Santos II, Barry Slate, Donna K. Teal, Zane Williard, Tazmen Carlisle, Kathy Coop, Marsha Heim, Lynette Dickerson, Mark Rainey, Amy Kirtley-Hill

76 Reproducible Writing Activities

www.themailbox.com

ISBN10 #1-56234-769-1 • ISBN13 #978-1-56234-769-7

Manufactured in the United States
10 9 8 7 6 5 4 3 2

Table of Contents

What's Inside

76 REPRODUCIBLE WRITING ACTIVITIES...

for independent work, center work, small-group work, and homework!

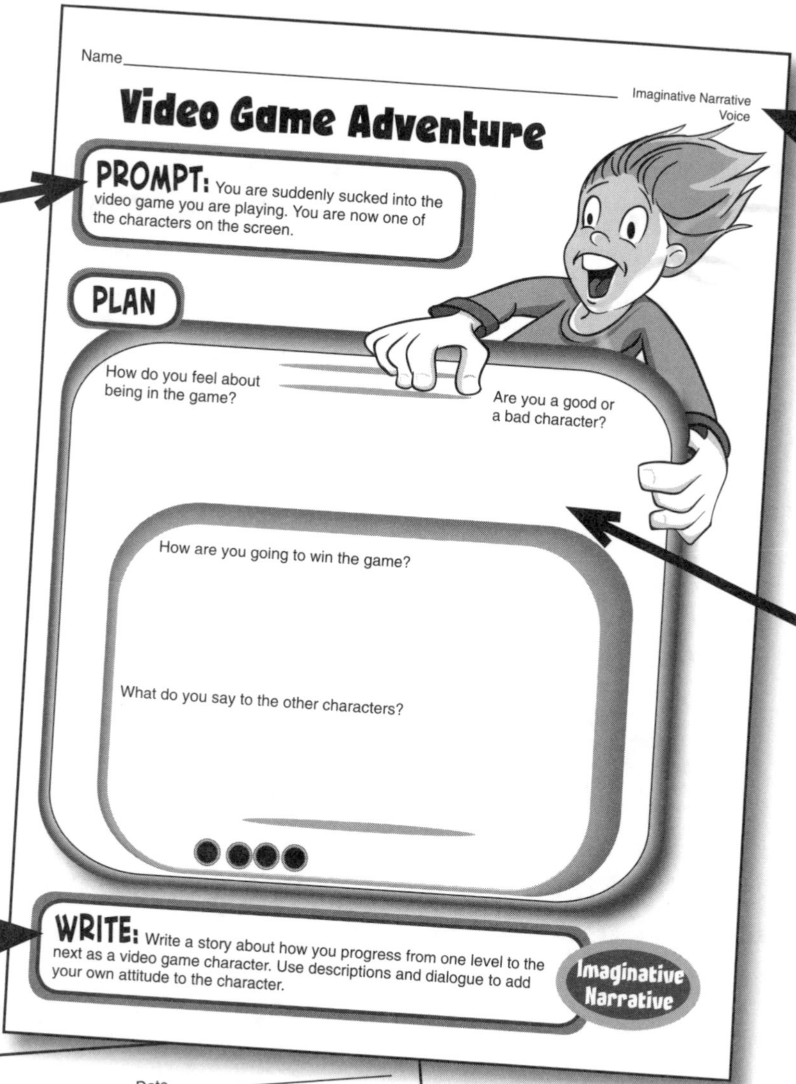

Name____________________

Imaginative Narrative
Voice

Video Game Adventure

PROMPT: You are suddenly sucked into the video game you are playing. You are now one of the characters on the screen.

PLAN

How do you feel about being in the game?

Are you a good or a bad character?

How are you going to win the game?

What do you say to the other characters?

WRITE: Write a story about how you progress from one level to the next as a video game character. Use descriptions and dialogue to add your own attitude to the character.

Imaginative Narrative

ENGAGING PROMPT

SKILL LINE SHOWING THE TYPE OF WRITING AND FEATURED SKILL

PREWRITING ORGANIZER TO HELP STUDENTS PLAN

WRITING TASK

Name____________________ Date____________

Writing Checklist

✓ AUDIENCE AND PURPOSE

___ uses correct tone for the intended audience

___ stays focused on the purpose of the essay

✓ ELABORATION

___ uses sensory details

___ uses descriptive language and vocabulary

✓ FLUENCY AND ORGANIZATION

___ thoughts are clear and well organized

___ transitions are smooth

___ essay is complete

✓ CONVENTIONS

___ uses varied sentence structure

___ uses correct grammar

___ uses correct capitalization and punctuation

___ uses correct spelling

AND, we've included an easy-to-use writing checklist on page 4.

Name_______________________________________ Date ______________________

Writing Checklist

✓ AUDIENCE AND PURPOSE

_____ uses correct tone for the intended audience

_____ stays focused on the purpose of the essay

✓ ELABORATION

_____ uses sensory details

_____ uses descriptive language and vocabulary

✓ FLUENCY AND ORGANIZATION

_____ thoughts are clear and well organized

_____ transitions are smooth

_____ essay is complete

✓ CONVENTIONS

_____ uses varied sentence structure

_____ uses correct grammar

_____ uses correct capitalization and punctuation

_____ uses correct spelling

Name_______________________________________ Date ______________________

Writing Checklist

✓ AUDIENCE AND PURPOSE

_____ uses correct tone for the intended audience

_____ stays focused on the purpose of the essay

✓ ELABORATION

_____ uses sensory details

_____ uses descriptive language and vocabulary

✓ FLUENCY AND ORGANIZATION

_____ thoughts are clear and well organized

_____ transitions are smooth

_____ essay is complete

✓ CONVENTIONS

_____ uses varied sentence structure

_____ uses correct grammar

_____ uses correct capitalization and punctuation

_____ uses correct spelling

Name ____

Top 'Toon

PROMPT: You have decided to write an essay to nominate your favorite animated cartoon show for "Cartoon of the Year."

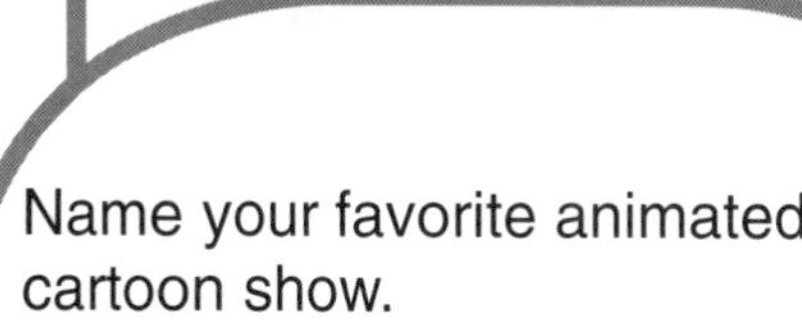

PLAN

How many judges do you think will read your nomination?

Do you think the judges are young or old? Explain.

What type of essay do you think they want to read?

Name your favorite animated cartoon show.

Briefly explain why you like the show.

WRITE: Describe to the judges the features that make your favorite animated cartoon show a good choice for "Cartoon of the Year." As you write, think about who the judges are and what they want to read.

Descriptive Writing

Name ____________________

WANTED

PROMPT: You and a friend have been hired by the FBI to find a missing person. You decide to write a description of him or her for the local television newscast.

PLAN

Missing Person

Introduction

Why are you writing?

What five words will grab the viewers' attention?

____________ ____________

____________ ____________ ____________

Description

Briefly describe the person you are looking for.

Conclusion

What should someone do if he or she finds the person?

WRITE: Write a news release about the FBI's missing person. Get your audience's attention in the introductory paragraph and be as descriptive as possible.

Descriptive Writing

Name____

Bus Stop Builders, Inc.

PROMPT: You are tired of standing in the wind, rain, and bitter cold at the bus stop. You decide to describe a new, perfect bus stop to your principal.

PLAN

Introduction

How can you grab the principal's attention?

Why are you writing to the principal?

Description

What will the new bus stop look like?

Conclusion

What is the most important reason for building a new bus stop?

WRITE: Write your plans for the perfect bus stop. Remember that a strong introduction gets the reader's attention and states what the essay is about.

Descriptive Writing

Name ____________________

The Place to Be Seen

PROMPT: It's your birthday. You've been asked to write an article about your party for a magazine column called "The Place 2 B Seen."

PLAN

The Introduction
Why should an article be written about your party?

The Information
Describe the party.

Sights

Sounds

Tastes

Smells

The End
What made your party extra special?

Birthday Girl

WRITE: Now write the magazine article. Be sure to write a strong introduction that makes other kids want to read about your party.

Descriptive Writing

Name____

PRIZED PAST

PROMPT: As you are cleaning your room, you find an old toy under your bed. You realize it has been there for eight years!

PLAN

What toy did you find?

What condition is it in?

What was it like when it was brand-new?

When did you last play with it?

What does it make you think of?

WRITE: Write about the toy you found under your bed. In the first paragraph, be sure to restate the prompt in your own words to form the main idea of the essay.

Descriptive Writing

Name

Getting Gorillas

PROMPT: The local zoo received a new gorilla from another zoo. As a student reporter, you have been allowed to see the exhibit before the rest of the public.

PLAN

What can visitors expect to see?	What might visitors hear in the exhibit?	How will the exhibit make visitors feel?

Main Idea

What is the most important thing about the exhibit that people should know?

WRITE: Write a newspaper article describing the zoo's newest attraction. Be sure to state in the first paragraph the most important thing about the exhibit.

Descriptive Writing

Name________________________________

A Madhouse

PROMPT: Your little brother invited ten of his friends to spend the night. They have made a mess of the whole house, including your room!

PLAN

Describe how the house looks overall.

Supporting Details

Describe the mess in the living room.

Describe the mess in the kitchen.

Describe the mess in your room.

WRITE: Describe the mess created by your brother and his friends. Be sure to include all the supporting details from above.

Descriptive Writing

Name ____

FROM WHERE I SIT

PROMPT: Your best friend moved away two days before school started. He or she is missing out on the coolest classroom ever!

PLAN

Describe the classroom to your friend in one sentence.

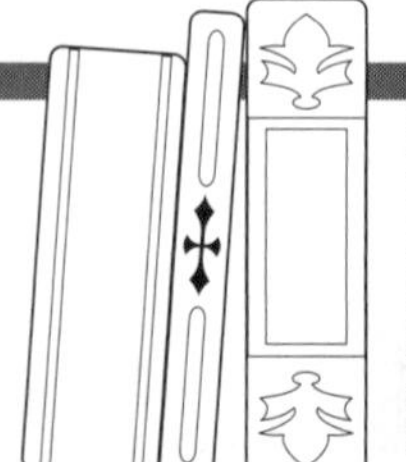

Now brainstorm a list of details about the classroom that support this sentence.

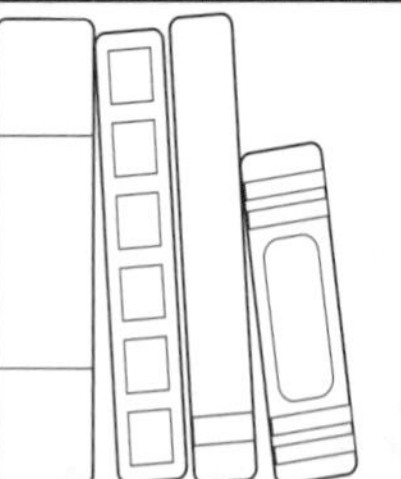

Write three sentences that describe the feelings you have when you are in class.

WRITE: Write a letter to your best friend describing your classroom. Use supporting details to help him or her understand exactly what it is like.

Descriptive Writing

Name ____________________

In Reality

PROMPT: Your best friend has been chosen to appear on TV in his or her own reality show set on a deserted island.

PLAN

Do you think your friend is a good choice for his or her own TV show?

Circle three of the following qualities that describe your friend and support your answer:

strong	weak	brave	quiet	afraid	serious
silly	smart	active	calm	tall	small
tough	other ________				

Explain why you chose the first quality circled.	Give an example of the second quality circled.	Use a comparison to describe the third quality circled.

WRITE: Write an essay describing why your friend would or would not make a good star for a reality TV show set on a deserted island. Use your notes above to support your opinions.

Descriptive Writing

Name____

One Smart Cookie

PROMPT: After taking a test, you prove that you are the smartest person on this planet.

PLAN

What was school like before the test?	What is school like after the test?
What was home like before the test?	What is home like after the test?
What were friends like before the test?	What are friends like after the test?

WRITE: Write an article for *Genius Quarterly.* Describe what your life was like before the test and what it is like after the test.

Descriptive Writing

Name____

International Air

PROMPT: Imagine that you are an astronaut aboard the International Space Station. You get to observe many unusual things in space.

PLAN

What objects do you **see** floating in space?

What does it **sound** like when objects hit the outside of the space station?

How does it **feel** to be weightless?

How does it **feel** to be so far away from family and friends?

WRITE: Write a journal entry for your daily travel log. Be sure to use your senses to describe your experience in outer space.

Descriptive Writing

Name____________________

The Scheme Machine

PROMPT: A mad scientist has created a super-scheme machine. He has set the dial and turned on the machine!

What scheme did the scientist set the machine to?

How long will this scheme last?

What does the world look like with this scheme in place?

What new sounds do you hear?

How does the mad scientist feel about his plans?

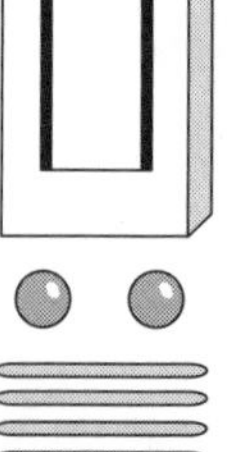

WRITE: From the mad scientist's point of view, write a journal entry describing the scheme and what it does to the world.

Descriptive Writing

Name ____________________

Creative Outlet

PROMPT: You have been hired to design a costume for a movie due in theaters this summer. The movie's director must approve your plans before you can get started.

PLAN

Name the main character and his or her role in the movie.

Draw a simple sketch of what the main character's costume should look like.

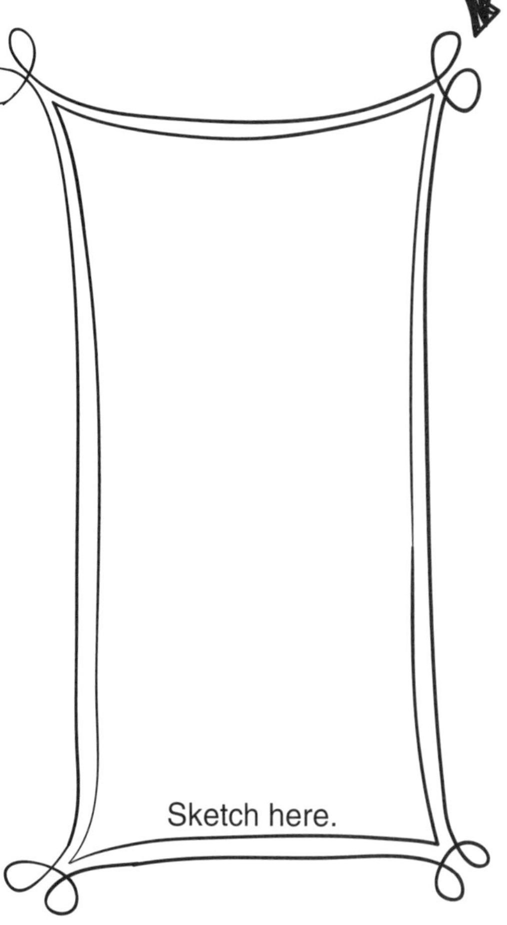

Describe the costume:

How does it look?

How does it feel?

How does it sound?

How does it smell?

WRITE: Write a description of the costume you plan to make. Be sure to use sensory details to help the director understand what you want to create.

Descriptive Writing

Name ____________________

X Marks the Spot

PROMPT: Imagine that you are following a treasure map to find gold and jewels. You decide to record in a journal what you see along the way.

PLAN

Start

Day 1

Animals:

Plants:

People:

Day 2

Animals:

Plants:

People:

Day 3

Animals:

Plants:

People:

WRITE: Use your notes to write a one-page journal entry describing what you see each day as you hunt for the buried treasure.

Descriptive Writing

Name____

Best Foot Forward

PROMPT: A major shoe company has just made you responsible for designing the next big shoe trend.

PLAN

1. What special features do you want on the shoe?

2. What materials are needed to make the shoe?

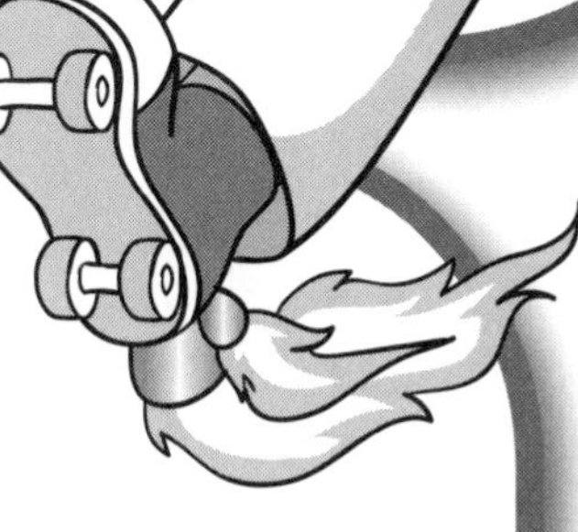

3. Who might be interested in buying the shoe? Why?

WRITE: Organize the information you recorded into a descriptive essay about the shoe you would design.

Descriptive Writing

Name____

Dangerous Detour

PROMPT: You and your classmates are on a safari in Africa when a terrible storm hits. Your tour guide takes you on a short but dangerous detour.

PLAN

Describe the safari bus you are in.

Describe student reactions to taking the detour.

Describe the animals seen on the detour.

Describe how you feel once the safari is over.

WRITE: Describe what it is like to go on a dangerous safari field trip. Organize the essay by the order in which you experienced each event or saw each animal.

Descriptive Writing

Name ____________________

RECORDING A RECORD

PROMPT: You have just set a new world record. The publisher of *Absolutely Amazing Records* would like you to write an article about your accomplishment.

PLAN

Absolutely Amazing Records

What record did you set?

How did you prepare to set the record?

How did you feel while you were setting the record?

How did you feel after you set the record?

What are some strong adjectives you can use in your article?

What are some strong adverbs you can use in your article?

WRITE: Write an article about your record-setting event. Use strong adjectives and adverbs to make your article more interesting.

Descriptive Writing

Name______________________________

THE FUN FACTOR

PROMPT: You and a group of friends have just walked through the fun house at the state fair for the first time.

PLAN

Something heard in the fun house:

____

Adjectives

Adverbs

Something else heard in the fun house:

____

Adjectives

Adverbs

Something seen in the fun house:

____

Adjectives

Adverbs

Something else seen in the fun house:

____

Adjectives

Adverbs

WRITE: Write an article that describes the fun house through the eyes of a first-time visitor. Use rich adjectives and adverbs to help readers feel the sights and sounds.

Descriptive Writing

Name ____________________

BORROWED BIKE?

PROMPT: You and your best friend rode your bikes to the zoo. All of a sudden, a monkey escaped on your bike. Now the police need some information.

PLAN

Use adjectives to describe your bike.

Color	Designs	Brand/Type of Bike
Size		

Use adverbs to describe how the monkey escaped on your bike.

How	When	Where

WRITE: Write a complete description of the incident for the police. Be sure to use strong adjectives and adverbs to describe your bike and how the monkey escaped on it.

Descriptive Writing

Name___________________________________

Mummy!

PROMPT: You have just helped discover a 10,000-year-old mummy in an Egyptian tomb. Now *Archaeologist Weekly* wants the scoop.

PLAN

Possible adjectives to use:

Possible adverbs to use:

Introduction:

Where were you when you found the mummy?

What did you first think when you saw it?

Details:

What did the Egyptian tomb look like?

What types of treasures were buried with the mummy?

Conclusion:

What will happen to the mummy now?

WRITE: Use the notes from above to write an article about your amazing discovery. Don't forget to use your lists of adjectives and adverbs to liven the story up a bit!

Descriptive Writing

Name____

Go, Team, Go!

PROMPT: Imagine that you are the coach of a sports team. Just before the biggest game of the season, you need to plan a team pep talk.

PLAN

What type of sports team are you going to talk to?

What kind of tone are you going to use? (Circle one.)

excited angry funny worried proud warm nervous helpful

Describe how the team has done so far this season.

Describe how the other team has done so far this season.

Describe what you want your team to do on the playing field.

WRITE: Write a pep talk to help motivate your team to victory. Remember to use your voice and tone to really get the players going!

Descriptive Writing

Name ______________________________

Crime-Scene Conclusions

PROMPT: All the sports equipment has been stolen from the school's gym. You have been sent to investigate the crime scene.

PLAN

Introduction

Describe the crime and what was taken.

Details

Describe the fingerprints found at the scene.

Describe the clothing fibers found at the scene.

Describe any other evidence left by the criminal.

Conclusion

Summarize the evidence found.

State who stole the sports equipment.

WRITE: Write about all your findings in the investigation. Be sure to include a strong conclusion that restates the main information as well as states who you think committed the crime.

Descriptive Writing

Name ___

Split Second

PROMPT: At the world's largest amusement park, you decided to ride the world's longest roller coaster.

PLAN

1. What did you think and feel as the ride began?

2. What words describe what you saw from the highest point of the ride?

3. What words describe the sounds you heard on the ride?

4. What did you think and feel as the ride ended?

5. Will you ever ride such a long roller coaster again? Explain.

WRITE: Write a description of the ride to give to the people who are still waiting in line. Remember that a good conclusion restates the main information.

Descriptive Writing

Name____

One Tough Tooth

PROMPT: Think about a time when you had a loose tooth that needed a little help falling out.

PLAN

Whom do you want to share your story with?

Who helped you with your loose tooth?

What were the events that happened?

-
-
-

How did you feel after the tooth came out?

WRITE: Write a story about your loose tooth. As you write, be sure to think about whom you are going to share your story with.

Personal Narrative

Name____

A Lesson Learned

PROMPT: Remember a time when you set a goal. Think about the lesson you learned from that experience.

PLAN

What goal did you set?

How did you try to reach the goal?

Were you successful? Explain.

What lesson did you learn from the experience?

WRITE: Write an essay about your goal-setting experience. Be sure to state the lesson you learned in the introduction to help grab the reader's attention.

Personal Narrative

Name ____________________

So Wrong!

PROMPT: Think about a time when a friend accused you of doing something that you would never do.

PLAN

What events took place before your friend accused you?

1.	2.	3.

Main Idea

What did your friend accuse you of doing?

How did this make you feel?

What events took place after your friend accused you?

1.	2.	3.

WRITE: Write your story as a journal entry. Remember to clearly state the main idea of the story.

Personal Narrative

Name________________________________

Running Late

PROMPT: Think about a morning when you overslept.

PLAN

How did your day begin?

What happened as a result of your oversleeping?

Event 1	Event 2	Event 3

How did your day end?

WRITE: Use strong supporting details to help you write a story about oversleeping one morning.

Personal Narrative

Name ____________________

Part of the Fun

PROMPT: Think about a time when you played a joke on someone.

PLAN

The Joke

What was the joke?

The Details

Who was involved?

How was the joke set up?

What happened while you were playing the joke?

What happened immediately after the joke was played?

WRITE: Write about a time when you played a joke on someone or someone played a joke on you. Be sure to explain the joke and why it was or was not funny.

Personal Narrative

Name ____________________

Remember When

PROMPT: Flash back to a time when you were asked to do something you did not think you could do, but you found out that you could.

PLAN

What were you asked to do?

Why did you not think you could do it?

Reason 1	Reason 2

Why did you decide to try it anyway?

Reason 1:

Reason 2:

WRITE: Write a letter to your family telling them about your experience. Be sure to share the details about why you did not think you could do it and why you tried it anyway.

Personal Narrative

Name ____________________

You Look a Little Green

PROMPT: Think about a time when you were jealous. Remember how you reacted in that situation.

WRITE: Write a magazine article titled "I Was Looking a Little Green." Be sure to state the main idea of the story and support it with plenty of details.

Personal Narrative

Name____

Best Friends

PROMPT: Remember a time when your best friend and you did something unexpected.

PLAN

Setting:

People involved:

First,

Then

Next,

Later,

After that,

Finally,

WRITE: Write a story about your best friend and you doing something out of the blue. Carefully retell the events in the order in which they occurred.

Personal Narrative

Name____

Trouble Is Brewing

PROMPT: Think about the first time you ever got in trouble. Remember where you were and what you were doing.

PLAN

Beginning

It all started

So then I

Middle

Next, I

After that, I

Ending

Finally, I

WRITE: Write a letter to the person you upset explaining the events that got you in trouble. Then close the letter by apologizing or asking for forgiveness.

Personal Narrative

Name ____

How Embarrassing!

PROMPT: Think of your most embarrassing moment. Replay it in slow motion in your mind.

PLAN

The setting and characters:

Events leading up to the embarrassing moment:

The moment of embarrassment:

Events after the embarrassing moment:

WRITE: Write about your most embarrassing moment. Be sure to write a story with a strong plot to keep readers interested.

Personal Narrative

Name____

A Winner!

PROMPT: Remember a time when you won a big game or contest. Think about the events that led up to and followed this exciting time.

PLAN

1. Introduction

2. Rising Action

3. Climax

4. Falling Action

5. Conclusion

FIRST PRIZE

WRITE: Write a journal entry about a time you won a game or contest. Focus on building the story until the climax and then writing a solid conclusion that answers all questions.

Personal Narrative

Name____

When You're Older

PROMPT: Think about the last time someone told you, "When you're older, you will understand." Think about the events that led up to the person saying this.

PLAN

Where and when did the events take place?	
What happened first?	What happened next?
What did you say?	What did the other person say?

WRITE: Write a journal entry that tells about the last time someone said you needed to be older to understand. Be sure to include plenty of dialogue that shows the moods and feelings of the characters.

Personal Narrative

Name ______________________________

What a Trip!

PROMPT: Think about a time when you had fun on a field trip that you thought would be boring.

PLAN

Where did you go on the field trip?	How did you feel before you left on the field trip?
What did you say to your friends about the trip before you left?	What made the field trip exciting?

What did you say to your friends while you were on the field trip?

What did they say about the trip?

WRITE: Now write an article about the field trip for your class yearbook. Include plenty of dialogue to keep readers interested.

Personal Narrative

Name____

Surprise!

PROMPT: Remember the best surprise you have ever experienced. Think about the amazing events that took place.

PLAN

What was the surprise?

What did you see that surprised you?

What sounds do you remember when you think about the surprise?

How did you feel?

What tastes or smells do you remember when you think about the surprise?

WRITE: Write about the time you were surprised. Be sure to include details for each of your senses: touch, taste, smell, sight, and hearing.

Personal Narrative

Name ____

Laugh Factory

PROMPT: Think about a time when you and a friend could not stop laughing.

PLAN

Ha Ha Ha Ha Ha

When and where did it all start?

What happened that made you start to laugh?

What happened when you could not stop laughing?

How did you finally stop laughing?

Strong adjectives to use in the story:

Strong adverbs to use in the story:

WRITE: Use strong adjectives and adverbs to write about your funny experience.

Personal Narrative

Name ____________________

Sick Day

PROMPT: Think about the last time you were too sick to go to school.

PLAN

Adjectives to use in your story:

Adverbs to use in your story:

When did you realize you were too sick to go to school?

What did you do next?

How did your day end?

WRITE: Write a note to your teacher explaining what you were doing while you were out sick. Be sure to use plenty of adjectives and adverbs to impress your teacher!

Personal Narrative

Name____________________

Just Picture It!

PROMPT: Remember a time when something so incredible happened that you wished you had a camera. Think about what a story that picture would have told!

PLAN

Describe what happened.

Who?

What?

When?

Where?

How did this event make you feel?

If you were to tell this story to a friend, what are some words or phrases you would use?

WRITE: Write a story about the incredible event. Let your emotions and personality show in what you write.

Personal Narrative

Name____

A Fun Trick!

PROMPT: Think about a time when you learned how to do an activity for the first time.

PLAN

1. What activity did you learn how to do?

2. How did you learn how to do this activity?

3. How did you feel once you learned the activity?

4. What are the benefits of learning this activity?

5. Do you still do this activity today?

WRITE: Write about the time you learned a new activity. Be sure to write a strong conclusion by stating your final opinion.

Personal Narrative

Name____

A Smash Hit!

PROMPT: Imagine that a famous movie company is looking for a new animated movie to make. You decide to send them your own idea for a movie.

PLAN

What do you know about animated movies?

What do you think the company is looking for in a movie?

What will your movie be about?

What lesson will kids learn by watching your movie?

WRITE: Write an imaginary story that you would like to see the movie company produce. Be sure to write a complete story that would appeal to the movie creators.

Imaginative Narrative

Name____

School in the Sky

PROMPT: You stop to wipe your feet on the school's doormat before entering the building. Suddenly, the mat magically flies you to a different school—a school in the sky!

What do you see as you fly through the air on the doormat?

Where in the sky is this school located?

Which of your classmates have also been taken to this new school?

How do you feel about being at a school in the sky?

WRITE: Write a story about your experience at this new school. Remember that the introductory paragraph should state the setting and explain to readers what is happening to you.

Imaginative Narrative

Name ____________________

When Lightning Strikes

PROMPT: Imagine there is a big thunderstorm one night. Every time lightning strikes during the storm, you become a different person.

PLAN

Who are the characters in your story?

Where does your story take place?

What is the main event that is going to happen in your story?

How is your story going to end?

WRITE: Write a story about your experience during this big storm. Be sure to only include information that supports your main idea.

Imaginative Narrative

Name ____________________

The One That Got Away

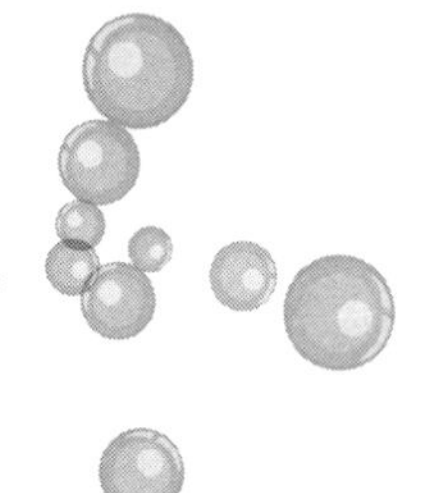

PROMPT: You are in a boat in the middle of a lake, fishing by yourself. You feel a tug on your fishing pole. As you peer over the edge of the boat, you are suddenly pulled underwater.

PLAN

A giant goldfish has pulled you underwater to its secret kingdom.

Supporting detail:

The goldfish begins to talk to you in a strange language.

Supporting detail:

You ask another fish passing by what the goldfish is saying.

Supporting detail:

You realize the goldfish needs help removing a rusty hook from its mouth.

Supporting detail:

WRITE: Write a story about a giant goldfish. Use the supporting details from above, plus any more you wish to add, to make the story more interesting.

Imaginative Narrative

Name______________________________

Who Needs Three Wishes?

PROMPT: A genie has granted your one and only wish. You are now a kid by day and an adult by night.

PLAN

What do you think about being both a kid and an adult?

What events in the story will support what you think?

Event 1

Event 2

Event 3

Event 4

WRITE: Now that the genie has granted your wish, write about your amazing experience. Use supporting details to make the story seem real to the reader.

Imaginative Narrative

Name________________________________

A Teeny, Tiny Story

PROMPT: You awake one morning to discover that all people are as small as ants. Plus, all ants are now six feet tall.

PLAN

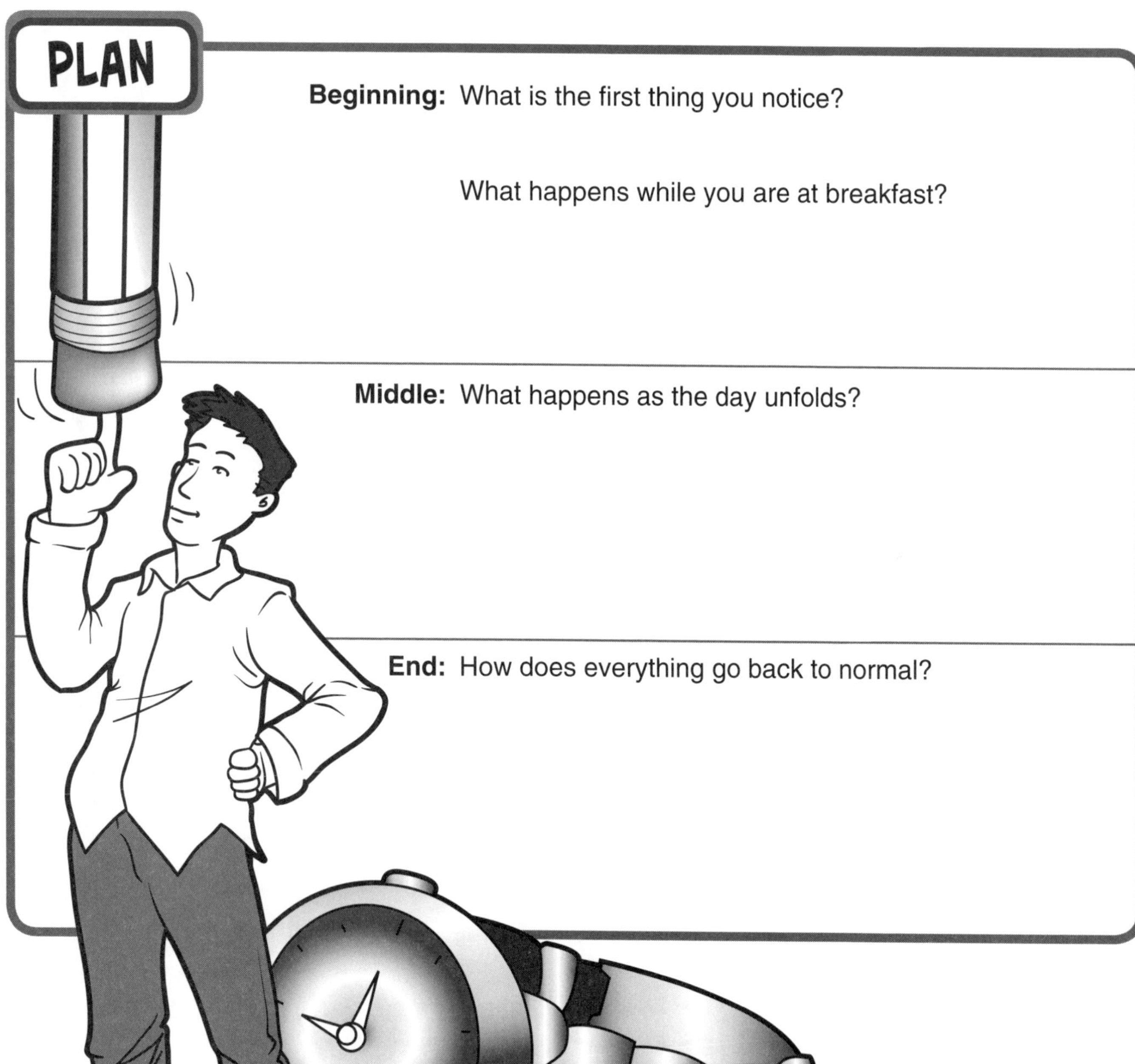

Beginning: What is the first thing you notice?

What happens while you are at breakfast?

Middle: What happens as the day unfolds?

End: How does everything go back to normal?

WRITE: Write a journal entry about your strange day. Remember to record the events in the order in which they happened.

Imaginative Narrative

Name____

Midnight Music Madness

PROMPT: You place your favorite CD in the player. But instead of hearing great music, you hear a mysterious voice, which gives you very specific directions.

PLAN

What does the voice tell you to do?

What do you do after you hear the directions?

As the story unfolds, what event changes everything?

How does the story end?

WRITE: Use the information above to help you write about your mysterious experience. Remember to include an introduction, exciting events, and a conclusion.

Imaginative Narrative

Name ______________________________

Castle Hassle

PROMPT: You are trapped in a castle that has no windows and no doors. A fire-breathing dragon is waiting for you in the tower.

PLAN

Introduction

Who:

Where:

Rising Action

Event 1:

Event 2:

Climax

Event 3:

Falling Action

Event 4:

Conclusion

WRITE: Use your imagination to tell the story of the time you were trapped in a castle. Follow the plotline from beginning to end.

Imaginative Narrative

Name____

Knock, Knock

PROMPT: Late one night, you hear a knock at your window. When you peer through the curtains to see what's making the sound, you cannot believe your eyes!

PLAN

What is at your window?

What does it want?

List two things it says to you.

List two things you say to it.

WRITE: Write about this strange night. Be sure to include plenty of dialogue between you and whatever is at your window.

Imaginative Narrative

Name ____________________

SUPERHUMAN SENSE

PROMPT: As you are watching one of your favorite TV shows, you notice something strange. One of your five senses is now 100 times stronger!

PLAN

Which of your five senses is now 100 times stronger? (Circle one.)

sight hearing smell taste touch

How does this improved sense make your life better?

How does this improved sense make your life worse?

WRITE: Use the details above to write a story about the day one of your senses became superhuman.

Imaginative Narrative

Name____________________

Busy Bee

PROMPT: Imagine that scientists have discovered a type of bee that does homework and chores. You decide to buy one on the Internet for $50.00.

PLAN

What happens when the bee arrives in the mail?

Are there any problems with the bee?

List strong verbs you can use in your story.

WRITE: Write a story about the bee you ordered on the Internet. Be sure to replace weak verbs with stronger ones.

Imaginative Narrative

Name____

Alien Sighting?

PROMPT: You are visiting your relatives in the country when aliens begin attacking the crops. You decide to call the police.

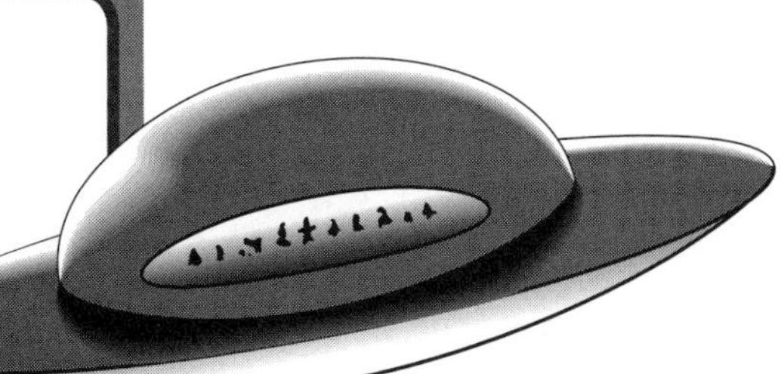

PLAN

Describe the aliens' clothes.

Describe how the aliens looked.

Describe how the aliens moved.

Describe the aliens' spaceship.

Describe how the spaceship moved.

WRITE: Write a letter home telling about the aliens' attack. Use plenty of adjectives and adverbs to help describe what happened.

Imaginative Narrative

Name____

Video Game Adventure

PROMPT: You are suddenly sucked into the video game you are playing. You are now one of the characters on the screen.

PLAN

How do you feel about being in the game?

Are you a good or a bad character?

How are you going to win the game?

What do you say to the other characters?

WRITE: Write a story about how you progress from one level to the next as a video game character. Use descriptions and dialogue to add your own attitude to the character.

Imaginative Narrative

Name ____

A Whole New World

PROMPT: Imagine that you have gotten on an airplane with your family. But as soon as you step off the plane, you step into a whole new world!

PLAN

What new world are you visiting?

What types of people live there?

Do you ever return home? Explain.

How will your adventure come to an end?

Will you ever fly again? Why or why not?

WRITE: Write a story about your bizarre plane trip to a strange world. In the conclusion, remember to answer any questions the reader may have.

Imaginative Narrative

Name________________________________

Happily Ever After

PROMPT: You are reading the story *Cinderella* to your little sister for what seems like the millionth time. You decide to change the ending to make it more interesting.

PLAN

Now hear ye, a funny ending:

Now hear ye, a scary ending:

Now hear ye, an ending with a simile:

Now hear ye, a surprise ending:

WRITE: Choose one ending from above to write a new conclusion to *Cinderella*.

Imaginative Narrative

Name____

Snake! Snake!

PROMPT: Your younger sister found a snake in the yard and wants to keep it as a pet. You decide to talk to your parents about it.

PLAN

How do you feel about having a snake in the house?

What are your parents' three biggest worries about pets?

-
-
-

Do you think your sister should be allowed to have a snake for a pet? Why or why not?

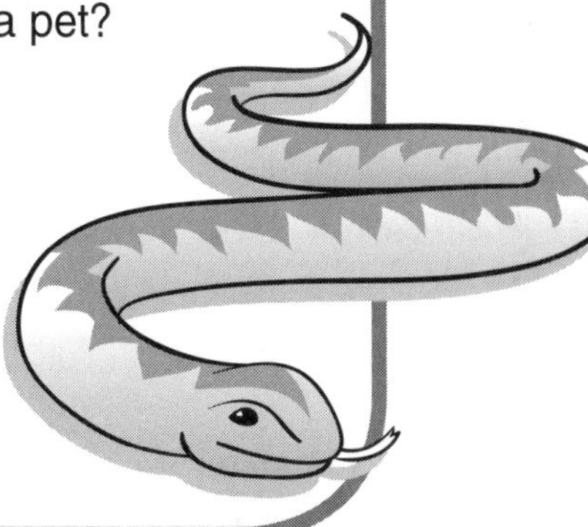

WRITE: Write a persuasive essay about keeping a snake as a pet. Remember to use arguments that will convince your parents to do what you want.

Persuasive Writing

Name ____________________

To Email or Not to Email?

PROMPT: Your principal is thinking about allowing students to have school email accounts.

PLAN

Are you for or against students having email accounts at school?

Think about some of the principal's concerns.

How will email affect student behavior?

How will email affect students' grades?

How will email affect the school's money?

WRITE: Keeping your principal's concerns in mind, write a persuasive email to him or her explaining why you should or should not have a school email account.

Persuasive Writing

Name____

Keeping It Healthy

PROMPT: Your school cafeteria has banned all junk food.

How do you feel about junk food?

How does the ban affect you?

Do you want the policy changed? Why or why not?

Who do you think needs to hear your opinions about the ban?

WRITE: Write a persuasive essay about the cafeteria ban. Use the information above to form a strong introduction that will get the reader's attention.

Persuasive Writing

Name____

The Price of a Playground

PROMPT: The school needs a new playground. The only land it can be built on is home to many rare plants and animals.

PLAN

Should the school build the playground?

What is the reason for your opinion?

List three facts that support your opinion.

-
-
-

WRITE: Write a letter to the editor of the local newspaper explaining your opinions about the playground project. Include a strong introduction that states your three facts.

Persuasive Writing

Name____

Too Much TV?

PROMPT: Some people say kids watch too much TV. Other people disagree.

PLAN

1. State which side you support.

2. What questions will the other side ask when confronted with your opinions?
   -
   -
   -

3. How will you answer these questions?
   -
   -
   -

WRITE: Use the questions and answers above to help you write a persuasive essay on the amount of TV kids watch each day.

Persuasive Writing

Name____

OPEN 24 HOURS

PROMPT: Some people believe that students should always be able to learn something—day and night. They want a school that is open to students 24 hours a day, seven days a week.

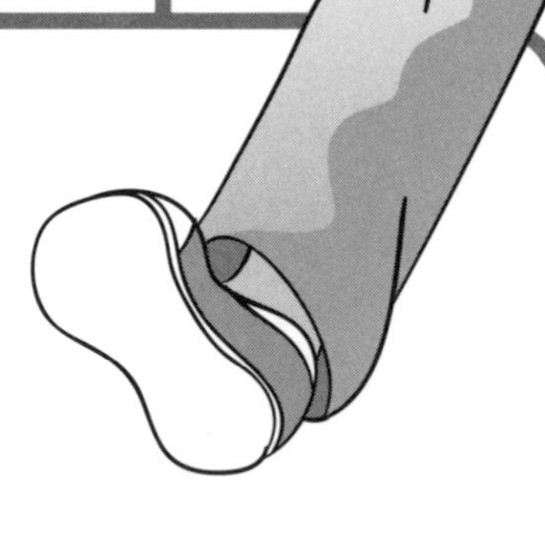

PLAN

State your opinion about this topic.

State your reasons for this opinion.

1.

2.

State the other side's opinion.

State the reasons for that opinion.

1.

2.

WRITE: Write a persuasive essay stating your opinion on school being open to students 24 hours a day, seven days a week. Be sure to support your opinion with strong facts and reasons.

Persuasive Writing

Name____________________

Team Spirit

PROMPT: Your favorite sports team is looking for someone new to wear its mascot costume. You know exactly who it should be.

PLAN

Who should be the new mascot?

Why should the team hire this person for the job?

•

•

•

How would this person help your favorite sports team?

WRITE: Write a letter to the owner of your favorite sports team. Explain to him why he or she should hire someone you know to be the new mascot.

Persuasive Writing

Name ______________________

Bubble Battle

PROMPT: A friend tells you that Bubble Bubble is the best chewing gum. You think Flavor Extreme is the best gum.

PLAN

What are the bad things about Bubble Bubble gum?

What are the good things about Flavor Extreme gum?

WRITE: Write a note to your friend to convince him that your gum is better than his. State the good things about your gum and remind him of the bad things about his gum.

Persuasive Writing

Name ____________________

Cancelled

PROMPT: The cable company wants to replace a cartoon channel with a 24-hour news channel.

PLAN

Think about the effect this will have on the following people:

Kids	Parents	Cartoon Artists
Effect:	Effect:	Effect:

WRITE: Write a letter to the cable company to convince it to either keep or replace the cartoon channel. Be sure to point out the effects replacing the channel would have on people.

Persuasive Writing

Name____

STRANDED

PROMPT: You and your family are stranded on a deserted island. You want to go exploring. The rest of your family wants to wait for help to arrive.

PLAN

How do you feel about being stranded?

What type of tone or attitude will you use to convince your family to go exploring (serious, funny, spooky, etc.)?

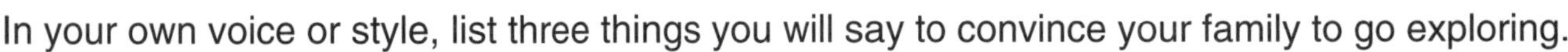

In your own voice or style, list three things you will say to convince your family to go exploring.

-
-
-

WRITE: Write a speech to convince your family to explore the deserted island. Choose your words carefully to make the speech sound like something you would actually say.

Persuasive Writing

Name____

Too Many Games!

PROMPT: Your best friend spends way too much time playing video games. You think he should get out of the house more.

PLAN

How much time does your friend spend playing video games?

What are some other things he could do with his time instead?

1.

2.

3.

How would his life improve if he played fewer video games?

Write one strong closing sentence that is sure to convince your friend to play fewer video games.

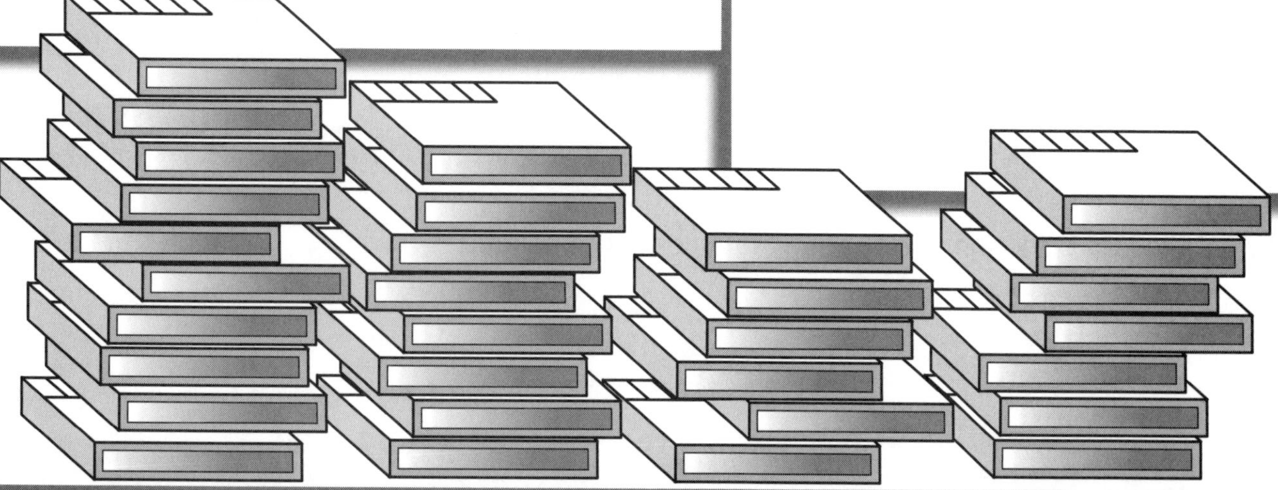

WRITE: Write a letter to your friend to convince him to play fewer video games. Be sure to end the letter with a strong statement that will get the reaction you want from him.

Persuasive Writing

Name ____

DON'T START!

PROMPT: You decide to tell someone about the dangers of smoking.

PLAN

Who are you going to tell about the dangers of smoking?

List five reasons that person should not smoke.

-
-
-
-
-

What fact about smoking do you want to leave the reader thinking about?

Write this fact in the form of a strong statement or question.

WRITE: Write a persuasive essay to convince someone that smoking is a bad habit. Include a final sentence that leaves the reader with a question or statement he must think about.

Persuasive Writing

Name____

HELPFUL HINTS

PROMPT: You have been asked to write an article for *The Third-Grade Reporter* titled "How to Survive Fourth Grade."

Who is your audience?

What type of information do you think they would like to read about?

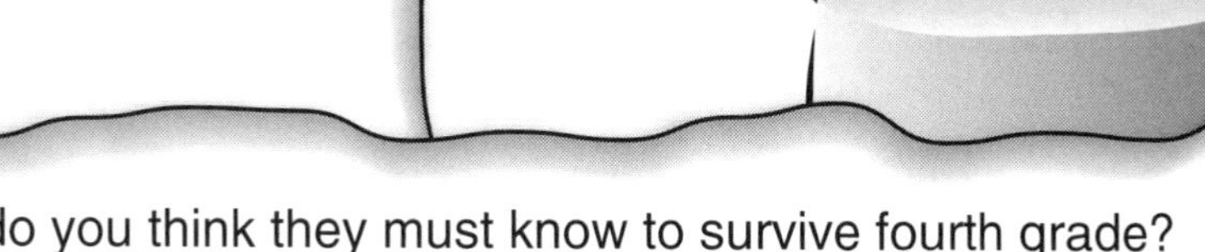

What information do you think they must know to survive fourth grade?

WRITE: Write an article about how to survive fourth grade. Remember who your audience is. Use words that the students can read and understand.

Expository Writing

Name______________________________

GET PLUGGED IN

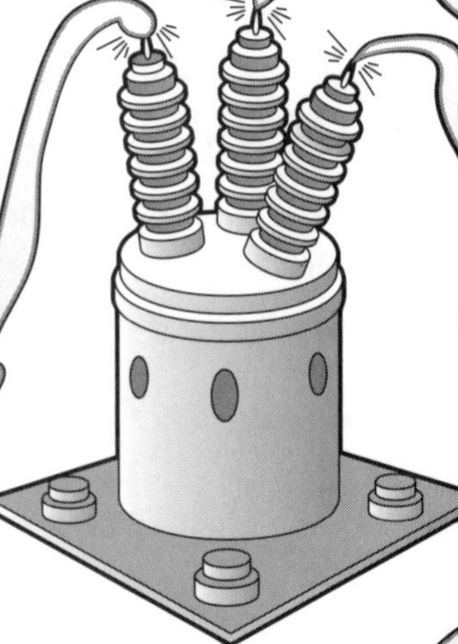

PROMPT: Your teacher challenged you to go all day without using electricity. Now that the day is over, you realize how much you like to use electricity.

PLAN

How do you feel about electricity?

What is one fact about electricity?

What items do you use that need electricity?

What would life be like without these items?

WRITE: Write about the importance of electricity in your life. In the first paragraph, state one fact and one opinion about electricity to gain the reader's interest.

Expository Writing

Name________________________________

License to Drive

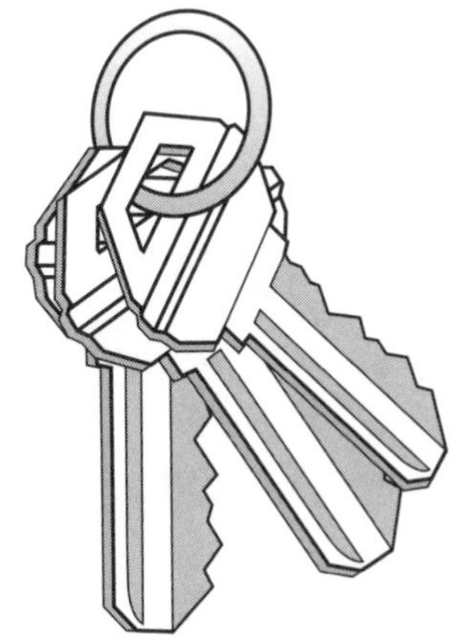

PROMPT: You are 16 years old. You are about to drive a car for the first time.

PLAN

Once you get in the car, what is the first thing you do?

What do you do next?

Then what do you do?

How do you stop the car and get out?

WRITE: Write an essay about how to safely drive a car. Be sure to keep the steps in order so as not to confuse the reader.

Expository Writing

Name ____

Who Are You?

PROMPT: Your teacher has a case of amnesia. He or she cannot remember how to do anything—including teach the class.

Complete the schedule based on what your teacher does during a normal school day.

Time	Activity/Lesson	Location

WRITE: Write a note reminding your teacher of what he or she does each day. Keep the events in order from the start of the school day until the last student leaves at the end of the day.

Expository Writing

Name____

What's Cool?

PROMPT: After your many years of playing with toys, a major toy company wants your opinion. It wants to know what toys are cool and what toys are for the birds.

PLAN

Cool Toys	Not-So-Cool Toys
•	•
•	•
•	•
•	•
•	•

What are your top three cool toys ranked in order?

What are your bottom three not-so-cool toys ranked in order?

WRITE: Write a toy report for the president of the company. Write about your top three cool toys first and then write about your bottom three not-so-cool toys.

Expository Writing

Name

Lifestyles of the Wealthy

PROMPT: Imagine that you are a millionaire. You want to explain to your butler exactly how you would like him to wait on you.

PLAN

What supplies will your butler need?

What will he do in the morning?

What will he do in the afternoon?

What will he do in the evening?

What transition words will you use?

WRITE: Use the list of transition words to help you write directions for your butler.

Expository Writing

Name ____________________

How to Be a Kid

PROMPT: Your parent is not quite up to speed on kids today. Explain to him or her what a typical day for a kid is like.

PLAN

What are the main events in the day of a kid?

-
-
-
-
-

Transition Words You Can Use

after
around
as soon as
finally
first
however
in conclusion
in the same way
lastly
next
second
then

WRITE: Use the events and transition words from above to write an essay explaining the typical day of a kid. Remember to place the events in the correct order.

Expository Writing

Name____

Let Me Tell You

PROMPT: You just found out that your best friend does not know anything about your favorite activity.

PLAN

What is your favorite activity?

Why is this your favorite activity?

How does this activity work?

Do you know of anyone else who does this activity?

Summarize what you have written so far.

Due Friday

WRITE: Write a note to your best friend telling him or her about your favorite activity. When writing the conclusion, be sure to summarize what you have written.

Expository Writing